TO:

FROM:

S0-AGV-529

Search me, O God,
and know my heart; test me
and know my anxious thoughts.
See if there is any offensive way in me,
and lead me in the way everlasting.

PSALM 139:23, 24

PRAYERS & BLESSINGS

Published by DaySpring Cards, Inc.
Siloam Springs, AR 72761 www.dayspring.com

Made in China

DECEMBER 30

May the Lord bless you
with more joys than you expected,
and greater gifts of His love
than you can imagine!

May you look forward to the year ahead with confidence in God— He loves you more than you can imagine, and cheers you on to fulfill His purpose for you.

Fear the Lord your God
and serve Him.
Hold fast to Him.

DEUTERONOMY 10:20

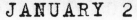

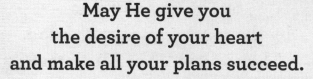

May He give you
the desire of your heart
and make all your plans succeed.

PSALM 20:4

Do not conform any longer
to the pattern of this world,
but be transformed
by the renewing of your mind.
Then you will be able to test
and approve what God's...
good, pleasing and perfect will.

ROMANS 12:2

May your walk with God
be closer than ever
and your spirit in tune with His will,
so that you will never
lose your footing or courage
along the path of life.

All that is good is yours
because of Jesus.
All that is fulfilling is yours
because you serve Him.
All that is peaceful is yours
because you love Him.

My help comes from the Lord,
the Maker of heaven and earth.
He will not let your foot slip—
He who watches over you
will not slumber.

PSALM 121:1-3

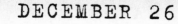

The gift of God is eternal life in Christ Jesus our Lord.

ROMANS 6:23

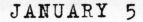

Your word is a lamp to my feet
and a light for my path.

PSALM 119:105

Thanks be to God for His
indescribable gift!

II CORINTHIANS 9:15

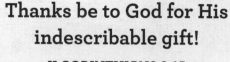

May you be blessed today, in a way that brings God's presence closer than you have ever known it.

His destiny was the cross...
His purpose was love...
His reason was *you*.
May the blessings of your day
be wonderful reminders
of all Jesus has given.

I pray that you,
being rooted and established in love,
may have power...to grasp
how wide and long and high and deep
is the love of Christ.

EPHESIANS 3:17-18 NIV

Glory to God in the highest,
and on earth peace to men
on whom His favor rests.

LUKE 2:14

May God
strengthen you with His love,
fill you with His assurance,
bless you with His peace,
and hold you in His arms
as you trust Him with every detail
of your day.

Jesus—
His birth was a signal of hope...
His life a reflection of God...
His heart an expression of love.
May you feel the depth of His love
in every part of your day.

Hope is the gentle 'lift' God gives our dreams while He prepares our hearts to see them come true— *may you never lose sight of the desires He's placed within you.*

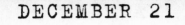

He hears the prayer
of the righteous.

PROVERBS 15:29

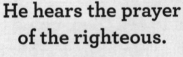

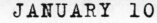

A longing fulfilled is a tree of life.

PROVERBS 13:12

He has given us
His very great
and precious promises.

II PETER 1:4

JANUARY 11

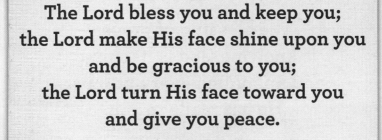

The Lord bless you and keep you;
the Lord make His face shine upon you
and be gracious to you;
the Lord turn His face toward you
and give you peace.

NUMBER 6:24-26

The blessing of prayer
is knowing God is listening,
and upholding every promise
He has made to you.

May God pour out
His blessings upon you—
Love and kindness;
Joy and laughter;
Peace and good things to come.

May He work in us
what is pleasing to Him,
through Jesus Christ,
to whom be glory for ever and ever.

HEBREWS 13:21

The blessing of the Lord
be upon you.

PSALM 129:8

Blessed are the pure in heart,
for they will see God.

MATTHEW 5:8

Surely, O Lord,
You bless the righteous;
You surround them
with Your favor as with a shield.

PSALM 5:12

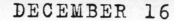

Lord, let my words be pleasing,
my actions be honoring,
and my life be glorifying to You
in every way.

May you see the 'just because' messages from God in your day: a timely word, a kindness, a warm smile, a favor, or anything that brings joy into your life.

We will be with the Lord forever...
encourage each other
with these words.

I THESSALONIANS 4:17, 18

Be blessed today:
There are no limits to God's love for you and what He can accomplish through you. He enjoys filling your life with goodness—it's the sweet reward of trusting Him.

We know that when He appears,
we shall be like Him,
for we shall see Him as He is.

I JOHN 3:2

Now to Him who is able to do immeasurably more than all we ask or imagine, according to His power that is at work within us, *to Him be glory.*

EPHESIANS 3:20-21

Glory to God
for the gift of Jesus...
Praise to God
for the joy of serving Him...
Thanks to God
for the hope of seeing Him.

May God Himself, the God of peace, sanctify you through and through.

I THESSALONIANS 5:23

Be joyful always; pray continually;
give thanks in all circumstances,
for this is God's will for you
in Christ Jesus.

I THESSALONIANS 5:16-18

Lord, please bless
the work of my hands today.
Let me be a true expression
of Your love, mercy, and joy.
May there be a light
shining from my spirit
that brings warmth to others
and glory to You.

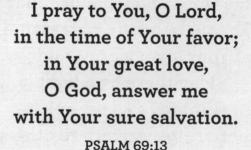

DECEMBER 11

I pray to You, O Lord,
in the time of Your favor;
in Your great love,
O God, answer me
with Your sure salvation.

PSALM 69:13

Let all who take refuge in You
be glad; let them ever sing for joy.
Spread Your protection over them,
that those who love Your name
may rejoice in You.

PSALM 5:11

May God's peace cover you,
His hope inspire you,
His joy uplift you,
His love surround you.

Send forth Your light
and Your truth,
let them guide me.

PSALM 43:3

If anyone is in Christ,
He is a new creation;
the old has gone,
the new has come!
All this is from God.

II CORINTHIANS 5:17, 18

Walk in peace today,
and allow God to lead you.
Serve with humility,
and allow Him to teach you.
Hope with confidence,
and allow Him to bless you.

DECEMBER 8

When the kindness and love of God
our Savior appeared, He saved us,
not because of righteous things we
had done, but because of His mercy.

TITUS 3:4, 5

May the God of hope
fill you with all joy and peace
as you trust in Him,
so that you may overflow with hope
by the power of the Holy Spirit.

ROMANS 15:13

When God gives you a gift,
it's eternally good—
and love is always
the reason He gives.

Praise be to the God and Father
of our Lord Jesus Christ,
Who has blessed us
in the heavenly realms
with every spiritual blessing
in Christ.

EPHESIANS 1:3

He is able to save completely those
who come to God through Him,
because He always lives
to intercede for them.

HEBREWS 7:25

Thank You, Lord,
for gray or busy days,
and even days when
everything seems to go wrong!
In those times we trust You to
brighten our lives with joy,
give us strength, and sustain us
with Your grace.

Christ Jesus, who died—more than
that, who was raised to life—
is at the right hand of God
and is also interceding for us.

ROMANS 8:34

May all who seek You
rejoice and be glad in You;
may those who love Your salvation
always say, "The Lord be exalted!"

PSALM 40:16

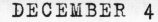

Be blessed today, and rejoice...
Jesus is praying for you!

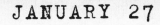

You who seek God,
may your hearts live!

PSALM 69:32

I praise You
because I am fearfully
and wonderfully made;
Your works are wonderful,
I know that full well.

PSALM 139:14

May the Lord remind you
that *He is for you,*
and nothing outside His will
can stand against you.
You are covered by forgiveness
and grace, loved, thought of
constantly, and chosen
to fulfill His divine purpose.

You are worthy, our Lord and God, to receive glory and honor and power, for You created all things, and by Your will they were created and have their being.

REVELATION 4:11

Teach me to do Your will,
for You are my God;
may Your good Spirit lead me
on level ground.

PSALM 143:10

May the spirit of God show you
how precious you are today—
and how carefully and wonderfully
you were made
for a special purpose.

If God is for us,
who can be against us?
He who did not spare His own Son,
but gave Him up for us all—
how will He not also,
along with Him,
graciously give us all things?

ROMANS 8:31, 32

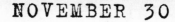

Seek first His kingdom
and His righteousness,
and all these things
will be given to you as well.

MATTHEW 6:33

The Lord bless you
with the riches of His grace;
the treasures of His love;
the comfort of His mercies;
the strength of His presence;
and the touch of His care.

Thank You, Lord,
for listening closely to my prayers,
seeing what my heart needs most,
and blessing my life
with Your goodness.

I pray that out of His glorious riches He may strengthen you with power through His Spirit in your inner being.

EPHESIANS 3:16

How great is the love
the Father has lavished on us,
that we should be called
children of God!

I JOHN 3:1

FEBRUARY 2

May your whole spirit, soul
and body be kept blameless at the
coming of our Lord Jesus Christ.
*The one Who calls you is faithful
and He will do it.*

I THESSALONIANS 5:23

Great is our Lord
and mighty in power;
His understanding has no limit.

PSALM 147:5

May the Lord's mercy make you feel like a new person today, ready to face everything that comes your way with a heavenly perspective.

Thank You, Lord, for the rewards of Your love and grace; for letting me discover Your will for my life with patience and understanding; for being a compassionate Father and constant friend.

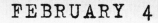

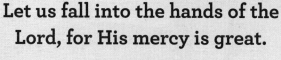

Let us fall into the hands of the
Lord, for His mercy is great.

II SAMUEL 24:14

Show that you are a letter
from Christ...written not with ink
but with the Spirit
of the living God,
not on tablets of stone
but on tablets of human hearts.

II CORINTHIANS 3:3

Let us be self-controlled,
putting on faith and love
as a breastplate,
and the hope of salvation
as a helmet.

I THESSALONIANS 5:8

Blessed are those who hunger
and thirst for righteousness,
for they will be filled.

MATTHEW 5:6

The Lord bless you with laughter,
a sound *He loves to hear.*
The joy of the Lord is your strength—
and the decision to walk
in that joy today
will cast a beautiful light
on God's goodness.

Thank You, Lord,
for the way You've blessed my life and
shown me how to be a blessing
to others.
Let my heart be a continual harvest
of kindness, generosity, joy,
and love.

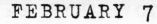

You make me glad
by Your deeds, O Lord;
I sing for joy
at the works of Your hands.

PSALM 92:4

Fan into flame the gift of God...for God did not give us a spirit of timidity, but a spirit of power, of love and of self-discipline.

II TIMOTHY 1:6, 7

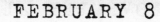

The joy of the Lord is your strength.

NEHEMIAH 8:10

Praise the Lord, O my soul,
and forget not all His benefits.

PSALM 103:2

May your day be filled with opportunities to love others, in ways that genuinely translate God's care for them even in the smallest ways.

Thank You, Lord,
for reminding me today
of the ways You've met my needs
in the past—reassuring my heart
of Your constant love
and faithfulness.

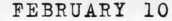

May the Lord make your love increase and overflow for each other and for everyone else.

I THESSALONIANS 3:12

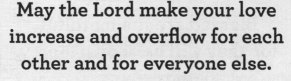

Blessed are the merciful,
for they will be shown mercy.

MATTHEW 5:7

I pray that you may be active
in sharing your faith, so that you
will have a full understanding
of every good thing
we have in Christ.

PHILEMON 1:6

Let your conversation
be always full of grace,
seasoned with salt,
so that you may know
how to answer everyone.

COLOSSIANS 4:6

God bless you with a grateful heart,
it is the source of humility;
God bless you with a joyful spirit,
it is the well of strength;
God bless you with a peaceful soul,
it is the reflection of trust.

Lord, make me keenly aware
of Your desire to bless
those around me today.
Give me all I need
to be Your vessel.

May the Lord of peace Himself
give you peace at all times
and in every way.

II THESSALONIANS 3:16

Save Your people
and bless Your inheritance;
be their shepherd
and carry them forever.

PSALM 28:9

I pray that you
may enjoy good health
and that all may go well with you,
even as your soul
is getting along well.

II JOHN 1:2

Those who hope in the Lord
will renew their strength.
They will soar on wings like eagles;
they will run and not grow weary,
they will walk and not be faint.

ISAIAH 40:31

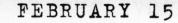

May your thoughts be on God today,
as His are on you *constantly*.

Thank You, Lord, for being
everything I need at all times—
I can count on You
to guard my steps,
bless the path ahead of me,
and carry me
when my strength is gone.

How precious to me are Your thoughts, O God!
How vast is the sum of them!
Were I to count them, they would outnumber the grains of sand.

PSALM 139:17, 18

Blessed are all who fear the Lord, who walk in His ways. You will eat the fruit of your labor; blessings and prosperity will be yours.

PSALM 128:1, 2

As the heavens are higher than the
earth, so are My ways higher
than your ways and My thoughts
than your thoughts.

ISAIAH 55:9

**Blessings crown
the head of the righteous.**

PROVERBS 10:6

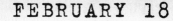

The Lord who loves you
and holds you in the palm of His hand
wants to bless you today—in amazing,
humbling, and breathtaking ways.

Thank You, Lord,
for priceless blessings—
the friendships You've created,
the family You've given,
the memories You've filled
with Your joy.

You are the rejoicing of God's heart.
May you feel His presence
as you go about your daily tasks
and share His love
with those He brings across your path.

Blessed are they...
who constantly do what is right.
Remember me, O Lord,
when You show favor
to Your people.

PSALM 106:3, 4

I pray also that the eyes of your heart may be enlightened in order that you may know the hope to which He has called you, the riches of His glorious inheritance.

EPHESIANS 1:18 NIV

Let us not become weary
in doing good,
for at the proper time
we will reap a harvest
if we do not give up.

GALATIANS 6:9

May all who seek You rejoice and
be glad in You; may those who love
Your salvation always say,
"The Lord be exalted!"

PSALM 40:16

Thank You, Lord, for the gift
of another day to love You,
praise You,
and serve You
with all my heart.

You are the recipient of *every promise* Jesus came to fulfill. He bridged the gap between you and God's blessings. May your steps take you in the direction of every good thing He has for you.

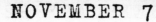

It is by grace you have been saved,
through faith—and this
not from yourselves,
it is the gift of God.

EPHESIANS 2:8

I keep asking that the God of our Lord Jesus Christ, the glorious Father, may give you the Spirit of wisdom and revelation, so that you may know Him better.

EPHESIANS 1:17 NIV

How much more
will those who receive
God's abundant provision of grace
and of the gift of righteousness
reign in life through the one man,
Jesus Christ.

ROMANS 5:17

Praise be to the God
and Father of our Lord Jesus Christ,
who has blessed us in the heavenly
realms with every spiritual blessing
in Christ.

EPHESIANS 1:3

Thank You, Lord, for the gifts
of Your grace—all the things
You give out of pure love,
abundant mercy,
and sweet forgiveness.

May God meet all your needs today. May the fulfillment be a reflection of His love, a revelation of His character, and a reminder that you are His—and you are *priceless*.

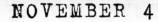

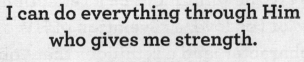

I can do everything through Him
who gives me strength.

PHILIPPIANS 4:13

My God will meet all your needs
according to His glorious riches
in Christ Jesus.

PHILIPPIANS 4:19

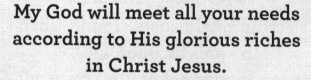

Thanks be to God,
who always leads us
in triumphal procession in Christ
and through us
spreads everywhere the fragrance
of the knowledge of Him.

II CORINTHIANS 2:14

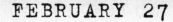

I have made you
and I will carry you;
I will sustain you
and I will rescue you.

ISAIAH 46:4

Thank You, Lord,
for giving me strength when I'm weary,
hope when I'm disappointed,
and peace when I'm anxious.

God lead you to the place where
trust leaves no room for worry,
and hope lifts you above every care.

You will be made rich in every way
so that you can be generous on every
occasion, and...your generosity
will result in thanksgiving to God.

II CORINTHIANS 9:11

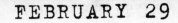

God loves you *perfectly;*
He forgives you *completely;*
He cares for you *constantly.*

Sovereign Lord, You have made
the heavens and the earth
by Your great power
and outstretched arm.
Nothing is too hard for You.

JEREMIAH 32:17

May integrity and uprightness
protect me,
because my hope is in You.

PSALM 25:21

It's never a question
of whether or not God will bless you—
it's a matter of having your faith
stretched out enough to receive the
incredible measure of goodness
God wants to pour into your life!

May Your unfailing love
rest upon us, O Lord,
even as we put our hope in You.

PSALM 33:22

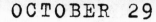

He chose us in Him
before the creation of the world
to be holy and blameless
in His sight.

EPHESIANS 1:4

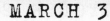

May God rekindle
the passion in your dreams,
and fill you with the desire
to see them come true.

The Lord has set apart the godly for Himself; the Lord will hear when I call to Him.

PSALM 4:3

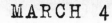

The desire of the righteous
ends only in good.

PROVERBS 11:23

Isn't it amazing
to know the God of the universe
set you apart to be His very own?
Let your heart celebrate
being held in His hands,
loved by His heart,
and cradled in His care.

May the Lord our God be with us...
may He never leave us nor forsake us.
May He turn our hearts to Him,
to walk in all His ways.

I KINGS 8:57, 58

The Lord bless you and keep you;
the Lord make His face
shine upon you
and be gracious to you;
the Lord turn His face toward you
and give you peace.

NUMBERS 6:24-26

The Lord bless you
with more hope than your heart can
hold...and use the overflow
to fill you with the courage
to do what you thought impossible.

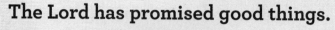

The Lord has promised good things.

NUMBERS 10:29

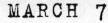

"If you can?" said Jesus.
"Everything is possible for him who believes."

MARK 9:23

The sunrise ushers in God's mercy toward you—yesterday is forgotten, today is in His hands, and tomorrow is filled with His promises.

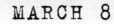

Nothing is impossible with God.

LUKE 1:37

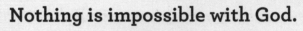

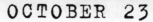

Lord, You establish peace for us; all
that we have accomplished
You have done for us.

ISAIAH 26:12

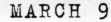

May your journey be showered
with the blessings of God,
and may they become road signs
that lead to His best.

Peace I leave with you;
My peace I give you.
I do not give to you as the world
gives. Do not let your hearts be
troubled and do not be afraid.

JOHN 14:27

**Teach me Your way, O Lord;
lead me in a straight path.**

PSALM 27:11

Let the blessings of the Lord
settle gently in your spirit today,
creating a beautiful place
for His joy to flourish.

Direct me in the path
of Your commands,
for there I find delight.

PSALM 119:35

You are my hiding place;
You will protect me from trouble
and surround me.

PSALM 32:7

God has prepared the day for you
and put His blessing upon it—
just because He loves you.

If we ask anything
according to His will, He hears us.
And if we know that He hears us—
whatever we ask—we know
that we have what we asked of Him.

I JOHN 5:14, 15

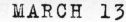

This is the day the Lord has made;
let us rejoice and be glad in it.

PSALM 118:24

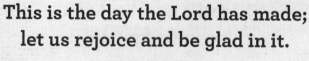

You are blessed because
you are in God's will—
His will is to heal you,
provide for you,
protect you,
and daily give you
the generous gifts of His grace.

I have loved you
with an everlasting love;
I have drawn you
with loving-kindness.

JEREMIAH 31:3

His divine power has given us
everything we need
for life and godliness
through our knowledge of Him.

II PETER 1:3

God bless you with courage
to do the extraordinary,
for He created you
with that in mind.

God has poured out His love
into our hearts by the Holy Spirit,
whom He has given us.

ROMANS 5:5

MARCH 16

I praise You because I am fearfully
and wonderfully made;
Your works are wonderful,
I know that full well.

PSALM 139:14

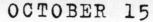

God's love is the most powerful,
life-changing force on earth—
may you allow it to flow freely
through you today.

No eye has seen,
no ear has heard,
no mind has conceived
what God has prepared
for those who love Him.

I CORINTHIANS 2:9

Serve the Lord your God
with all your heart
and with all your soul.

DEUTERONOMY 10:12

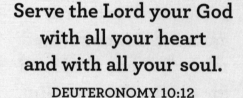

May your day begin and end
with a peaceful sense
of the Lord's presence...
a quiet heart...
and a thankful spirit.

In the morning, O Lord,
You hear my voice;
in the morning I lay
my requests before You
and wait in expectation.

PSALM 5:3

You have made known to me
the path of life; You will fill me
with joy in Your presence,
with eternal pleasures
at Your right hand.

PSALM 16:11

Lord, let me be overjoyed
to serve You today—there's nothing
more worthy of my time,
more nourishing to my soul,
or more satisfying to my spirit.

The Lord is near.
Do not be anxious about anything,
but in everything,
by prayer and petition,
with thanksgiving,
present your requests to God.

PHILIPPIANS 4:5, 6

As for God, His way is perfect;
the word of the Lord is flawless.
a shield for all
who take refuge in Him.

II SAMUEL 22:31

May the Lord abundantly bless your hopes and dreams, bring blessings out of your trials and challenges, and bless others through your hands and heart.

Let us hold unswervingly
to the hope we profess,
for He who promised is faithful.

HEBREWS 10:23

Let your light shine before men,
that they may see your good deeds
and praise your Father in heaven.

MATTHEW 5:16

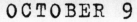

God cannot break a single promise
He's made to you—
and every one of them was written
to bless you.

We know that in all things
God works for the good of those
who love Him, who have been called
according to His purpose.

ROMANS 8:28

Because of His great love for us,
God, who is rich in mercy,
made us alive with Christ.

EPHESIANS 2:4, 5

May your day be filled
with a new appreciation
for serving God, and blessed
with a thankfulness
for all He has done
for others through you.

It is good to praise the Lord
and make music to Your name,
O Most High, to proclaim
Your love in the morning
and Your faithfulness at night.

PSALM 92:1, 2

I will bless you...
and you will be a blessing.

GENESIS 12:2

As you face a new day,
God wants to bless you.
He wants you to have joy, peace,
hope, and most of all,
the inexpressible comfort
of His love.

Whatever you do,
whether in word or deed,
do it all in the name of the Lord Jesus,
giving thanks to God the Father
through Him.

COLOSSIANS 3:17

He who did not spare His own Son,
but gave Him up for us all—
how will He not also,
along with Him,
graciously give us all things?

ROMANS 8:32

May you be blessed today—
blessed in a way that assures you of
the plans God has for your life.

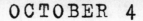

I will not forget you!
See, I have engraved you
on the palms of My hands.

ISAIAH 49:15, 16

"I know the plans I have for you," declares the Lord, "plans to prosper you and not to harm you, plans to give you hope and a future."

JEREMIAH 29:11

May you know how deeply
God desires to bless you—
His love is unconditional,
His promises are infallible,
and the good things
He has planned for you
are unstoppable.

The plans of the Lord stand firm forever, the purposes of His heart through all generations.

PSALM 33:11

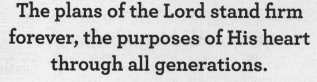

You, O Sovereign Lord,
have spoken,
and with Your blessing
of Your servant
will be blessed forever.

II SAMUEL 7:29

May you be blessed today,
in a way that fills your heart
with a thousand "thank-yous"
for all that God's hand
will bring your way.

Find rest, O my soul, in God alone;
my hope comes from Him.

PSALM 62:5

It is He who made us,
and we are His ;
we are His people,
the sheep of His pasture.
Enter His gates with thanksgiving
and His courts with praise.

PSALM 100:3, 4

Lord, help me to rest in You,
keep a quiet heart, and look forward
with hopeful expectation
to the things You are working
together for good.

There is blessing
in following your heart—
God works out His will for your life
through the desires He puts there.

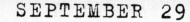

He will not let your foot slip—
He who watches over you
will not slumber.

PSALM 121:3

I will praise the Lord, who counsels me;
even at night my heart instructs me.

PSALM 16:7

All the days ordained for me
were written in Your book
before one of them came to be.

PSALM 139:16

May the words of my mouth
and the meditation of my heart
be pleasing in Your sight, O Lord,
my Rock and my Redeemer.

PSALM 19:14

Lord, it's so comforting to know
You never turn away from me.
In every moment Your hand
is at work designing
what is best for my life.

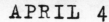

You are blessed by the Lord
moment by moment; for with every
breath we have an opportunity
to praise Him, serve Him, love Him.

Lord, You are our Father.
We are the clay, You are the potter;
we are all the work of Your hand.

ISAIAH 64:8

APRIL 5

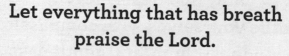

Let everything that has breath praise the Lord.

PSALM 150:6

As God's chosen people,
holy and dearly loved,
clothe yourselves with compassion,
kindness, humility, gentleness
and patience.

COLOSSIANS 3:12

The blessing of the Lord brings wealth, and He adds no trouble to it.

PROVERBS 10:22

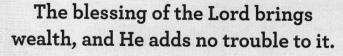

You are blessed
because you belong to God—
He chose you,
shaped you,
and prepared you
to make a difference
in the world.

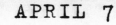

God's desire to bless you
is as great as He is...
and impossible to fathom.

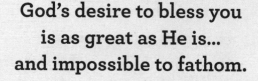

When you pass through the waters,
I will be with you;
and when you
pass through the rivers,
they will not sweep over you.

ISAIAH 43:2

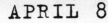

As high as the heavens are above the earth, so great is His love for those who fear Him.

PSALM 103:11

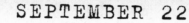

Do not be afraid, for I am with you.

ISAIAH 43:5

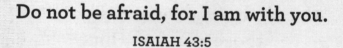

Whoever gives heed to instruction prospers, and blessed is he who trusts in the Lord.

PROVERBS 16:20

Lord, I pray for a fresh sense
of Your presence
in everything I do—
a sweet reminder that Your mercies
are new every morning
and Your love is boundless.

You have a special place
in God's plan—may your steps
be ordered by Him
and blessed with peace today.

He guides me
in paths of righteousness
for His name's sake.

PSALM 23:3

The Lord your God
will bless you as He has promised.

DEUTERONOMY 15:6

He guides the humble
in what is right
and teaches them His way.

PSALM 25:9

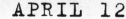

May you enjoy
the work before you today,
approaching it as if God is the only
One you're working for.

May you be blessed
in all you do today,
confident that the spirit of God
leads you with wisdom and love.

Whatever you do,
work at it with all your heart,
as working for the Lord...
since you know that you will receive
an inheritance from the Lord
as a reward.

COLOSSIANS 3:23, 24

Light is shed upon the righteous
and joy on the upright in heart.

PSALM 97:11

God will bless you
in all your work
and in everything
you put your hand to.

DEUTERONOMY 15:10

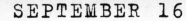

We, who with unveiled faces
all reflect the Lord's glory,
are being transformed
into His likeness.

II CORINTHIANS 3:18

God bless you with an enthusiasm for the purpose you were created to fulfill—and a fresh sense of knowing how important it is.

Today Lord, I trust You
to open my eyes and heart
to the needs of those around me—
and more than anything else,
I pray they see You in me.

Many are the plans in a man's heart,
but it is the Lord's purpose
that prevails.

PROVERBS 19:21

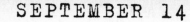

The Lord is my strength
and my shield;
my heart trusts in Him,
and I am helped.

PSALM 28:7

Rejoice in all the good things the
Lord your God has given to you.

DEUTERONOMY 26:11

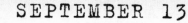

It is God who arms me
with strength
and makes my way perfect.

PSALM 18:32

May your trials lead you
to a closer relationship with God,
and become a threshold for even
greater blessings in your life.

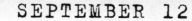

Our strength may fail,
but our God will not—
may He give you peace
of heart and mind today.

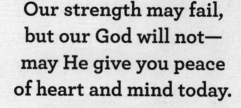

Blessed is the man who perseveres under trial, because when he has stood the test, he will receive the crown of life that God has promised to those who love Him.

JAMES 1:12

By day the Lord directs His love,
at night His song is with me—
a prayer to the God of my life.

PSALM 42:8

APRIL 20

The same Lord is Lord of all and richly blesses all who call on Him.

ROMANS 10:12

Blessed is he...whose hope is in the Lord his God.

PSALM 146:5

May the Lord give you an unwavering confidence that you can do anything He calls you to do, and it will be *blessed*.

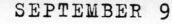

Prayer is the powerful connection
between our needs and our God—
and He is always more than enough.

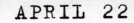

I have trusted in the Lord
without wavering.

PSALM 26:1

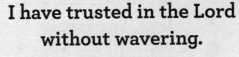

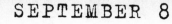

Look on me and answer,
O Lord my God.
Give light to my eyes.

PSALM 13:3

APRIL 23

The Lord will be your confidence
and will keep your foot
from being snared.

PROVERBS 3:26

Blessed are those
who have learned to acclaim You,
who walk in the light
of Your presence, O Lord.

PSALM 89:15

Wisdom is a blessing—
walk in it;
joy is a gift—
be generous with it;
prayer is a privilege—
act on it;
love is a miracle—
be God's messenger.

Lord, let me reflect the light
of Your love to those
who cross my path today,
because I know You planned
for our lives to touch.

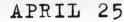

Teach us to number our days aright,
that we may gain a heart of wisdom.

PSALM 90:12

The eternal God is your refuge,
and underneath
are the everlasting arms.

DEUTERONOMY 33:27

The only thing that counts is faith expressing itself through love.

GALATIANS 5:6

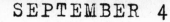

Great is Your love,
reaching to the heavens;
Your faithfulness
reaches to the skies.

PSALM 57:10

Be blessed with a quiet heart today—God is taking care of everything that concerns you.

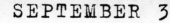

You are a masterpiece of God—
filled with purpose, eternally
valued, infinitely loved.

A heart at peace
gives life to the body.

PROVERBS 14:30

The Lord is faithful,
and He will strengthen
and protect you.

II THESSALONIANS 3:3

The Lord will guide you always;
He will satisfy your needs
in a sun-scorched land
and will strengthen your frame.

ISAIAH 58:11

He is the faithful God,
keeping His covenant of love
to a thousand generations
of those who love Him.

DEUTERONOMY 7:9

Joy comes from a deep-seated trust that God is in control of everything that concerns you—may you walk through your day knowing every need you have is met in full.

God is faithful, and He knows
the unspoken needs of your heart.
You can rest in the assurance
that He'll meet them on time—
and *generously*.

Look at the birds of the air;
they do not sow or reap or store
away in barns, and yet your
heavenly Father feeds them.
Are you not much more valuable
than they?

MATTHEW 6:26 NIV

Be still, and know that I am God.

PSALM 46:10

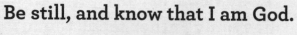

The Lord protects the
simplehearted;
when I was in great need,
He saved me.

PSALM 116:6

**In quietness and trust
is your strength.**

ISAIAH 30:15

May God bless you with wisdom
in each decision, strength in each
responsibility, success in each
endeavor, joy in each commitment,
peace in each relationship,
and love in everything!

AUGUST 28

The work the Lord wants you to do
is revealed in the stillness
of trusting in Him.

Who is wise and understanding among you? Let him show it by his good life, by deeds done in the humility that comes from wisdom.

JAMES 3:13

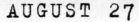

Those who know Your name
will trust in You, for You, Lord,
have never forsaken
those who seek You.

PSALM 9:10

If any of you lacks wisdom,
he should ask God, who gives
generously to all without finding
fault, and it will be given to him.

JAMES 1:5

Cast your cares on the Lord
and He will sustain you;
He will never let the righteous fall.

PSALM 55:22

May your heart always
know the Lord...
May your feet always
follow His path...
May your life always be
blessed by Him!

You will be blessed when you hope,
You will be blessed when you trust,
You will be blessed when you cast
All your cares on the Lord.

Create in me a pure heart, O God, and renew a steadfast spirit within me.

PSALM 51:10

God did not give us
a spirit of timidity,
but a spirit of power,
of love and
of self-discipline.

II TIMOTHY 1:7

Trusting the God of every blessing,
Who is good in every way,
To rest His hand upon you
And bring you joy today.

May the Lord direct your hearts
into God's love
and Christ's perseverance.

II THESSALONIANS 3:5

You open Your hand and satisfy the desires of every living thing.

PSALM 145:16

You are a priceless vessel
of the love God wants the world to see—
may you take every opportunity
He gives you to express it.

You hem me in—behind and before;
You have laid Your hand upon me.

PSALM 139:5

I will boast all the more gladly
about my weaknesses,
so that Christ's power
may rest on me.

II CORINTHIANS 12:9

May the blessings of the Lord be
upon you, dwell within you,
and flow through you.

The Lord saves His anointed;
He answers him
from His holy heaven
with the saving power
of His right hand.

PSALM 20:6

Whoever believes in Me,
as the Scripture has said,
streams of living water
will flow from within him.

JOHN 7:38

Praying you are strong in the Lord and the power of His might today— leaving every detail to Him.

If you remain in Me and My words remain in you, ask whatever you wish, and it will be given you. This is to My Father's glory, that you bear much fruit.

JOHN 15:7, 8

The Lord will fulfill His purpose
for me; Your love, O Lord, endures
forever—do not abandon
the works of Your hands.

PSALM 138:8

Praying that our Lord,
who loves you so dearly,
will speak blessings
and comfort to your heart today.

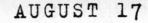

My purpose will stand,
and I will do all that I please.

ISAIAH 46:10

My shield is God Most High,
who saves the upright in heart.

PSALM 7:10

The moment you were born,
God awakened the purpose He put
within you—and He is attentive to
that purpose every day of your life.

Test me, O Lord, and try me,
examine my heart and my mind;
for Your love is ever before me, and
I walk continually in Your truth.

PSALM 26:2-3

Glorify the Lord with me;
let us exalt His name together.

PSALM 34:3

Today and always,
may you experience
God's love and joy...
and may your life be filled
with the blessings
of His goodness and grace.

I will praise You, O Lord my God,
with all my heart;
I will glorify Your name forever.

PSALM 86:12

From the fullness of His grace
we have all received
one blessing after another.

JOHN 1:16

Life is God's precious gift to you—
may you spend it
bringing glory to Him.

MAY 19

God is able to make all grace
abound to you,
so that in all things at all times,
having all that you need,
you will abound in every good work.

II CORINTHIANS 9:8

Guide me in Your truth
and teach me,
for You are God my Savior,
and my hope is in You
all day long.

PSALM 25:5

God has blessed you with the ability to achieve your goals, the courage to pursue your dreams, and the faith to believe in His promises.

Show me Your ways, O Lord,
teach me Your paths.

PSALM 25:4

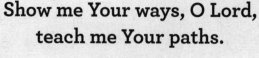

Let us fix our eyes on Jesus, the
author and perfecter of our faith.

HEBREWS 12:2

God would like to use today
to teach you more about His love
for you and His plan for your life—
may your heart be humble
and ready to learn.

Be strong and courageous...for the
Lord your God goes with you;
He will never leave you
nor forsake you.

DEUTERONOMY 31:6

Neither height nor depth,
nor anything else in all creation,
will be able to separate us
from the love of God that is in
Christ Jesus our Lord.

ROMANS 8:39

The Lord's thoughts and His heart
are toward you today— to keep you,
to guide you, and to bless you as
only He can.

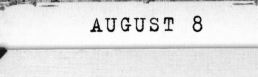

Do everything in love.

I CORINTHIANS 16:14

The Lord will keep you
from all harm—
He will watch over your life.

PSALM 121:7

Love is a choice,
a commitment,
an action,
a gift—
may the spirit of God give you
wisdom to follow your heart in the
way of love today.

Blessed are they who keep
His statutes and seek Him
with all their heart.

PSALM 119:2

The Lord is faithful
to all His promises
and loving toward all He has made.

PSALM 145:13

God chose you and drew you to His side. He called you and equipped you for His work.
He blessed you and gifted you to fulfill His purposes.

You know with all your heart and soul that not one of all the good promises the Lord your God gave you has failed.
Every promise has been fulfilled.

JOSHUA 23:14

MAY 27

Great and powerful God,
whose name is the Lord Almighty,
great are Your purposes
and mighty are Your deeds.

JEREMIAH 32:18, 19

Expect your life to be blessed—
it's impossible for God
to break His promises to you!

I cry out to God Most High, to God,
who fulfills His purpose for me.

PSALM 57:2

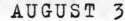

Praise Him for His acts of power;
praise Him for His
surpassing greatness.

PSALM 150:2

May the Lord bless you with all the
things that will assure you
of His love, His presence,
and His daily care for you.

I will remember
the deeds of the Lord;
yes, I will remember
Your miracles of long ago.

PSALM 77:11

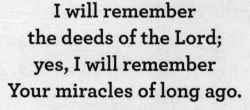

Let us not love with words or tongue but with actions and in truth. This then is how...we set our hearts at rest in His presence.

I JOHN 3:18, 19

Let yourself believe
in great things—
God is in the habit
of making them happen.

May today remind you
that God has given you a fresh start,
a new hope, and a heart *filled* with
reasons to be thankful.

You have taken off your old self
with its practices
and have put on the new self,
which is being renewed in knowledge
in the image of its Creator.

COLOSSIANS 3:9, 10

His compassions never fail.
They are new every morning.

LAMENTATIONS 3:22, 23

You were created in God's image—
may your actions
be a reflection of His love today.

Do not be anxious about anything, but in everything, by prayer and petition, with thanksgiving, present your requests to God.

PHILIPPIANS 4:6

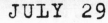

May you be blessed by the Lord,
the Maker of heaven and earth.

PSALM 115:15

May your day be blessed with the wonderful assurance of knowing that in you, God created someone very special.

Being confident of this,
that He who began
a good work in you
will carry it on to completion
until the day of Christ Jesus.

PHILIPPIANS 1:6

JUNE 4

Blessings crown the head
of the righteous.

PROVERBS 10:6

May the Lord fill you with
confidence today—
you are *His*,
you are *valuable*,
you are *blessed*.

JUNE 5

May the Lord bless you...all the days
of your life.

PSALM 128:5

O Lord, our Lord,
how majestic is Your name
in all the earth! You have set
Your glory above the heavens.

PSALM 8:1

In all things, may Jesus be
the strength of your heart,
the center of your life,
the guide of your future,
the joy of your soul.

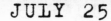

O Lord? Who is like You—
majestic in holiness,
awesome in glory,
working wonders?

EXODUS 15:11

Love the Lord your God
with all your heart
and with all your soul
and with all your strength.

DEUTERONOMY 6:5

There isn't a moment of your day
left to chance—each one
has been set into motion by God
for the blessing of your good
and His glory.

He will command His angels
concerning you to guard you in all
your ways; they will lift you up in
their hands, so that you will
not strike your foot against a stone.

PSALM 91:11, 12

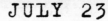

**Thanks be to God!
He gives us the victory
through our Lord Jesus Christ.**

I CORINTHIANS 15:57

May God bless you
with good health,
protect you
with His almighty strength,
and keep you
always in His tender care.

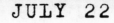

With God we will gain the victory.

PSALM 108:13

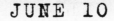

I am the Lord, who heals you.

EXODUS 15:26

May God give you fresh dreams,
new victories, and endless joys...
in surprising ways, unexpected
blessings and overflowing measure!

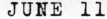

Do not withhold Your mercy from me, O Lord; may Your love and Your truth always protect me.

PSALM 40:11

The peace of God,
which transcends all understanding,
will guard your hearts and your minds
in Christ Jesus.

PHILIPPIANS 4:7

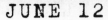

The Lord has
a purpose for you to fulfill,
the power to equip you,
and strength to uphold you.

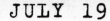

May God's blessings be multiplied
to you today—abundant life,
pure love, and perfect peace.

Be strong in the Lord
and in His mighty power.

EPHESIANS 6:10

Be joyful in hope,
patient in affliction,
faithful in prayer.

ROMANS 12:12

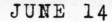

The name of the Lord
is a strong tower;
the righteous run to it
and are safe.

PROVERBS 18:10

JULY 17

May the righteous be glad
and rejoice before God;
may they be happy and joyful.

PSALM 68:3

When the Lord adds
His blessing to your life,
there's no limit to your success!

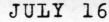

May your life always be abundant—
in joyful service, in daily blessings,
in abiding love.

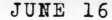

JUNE 16

Commit to the Lord whatever you do, and your plans will succeed.

PROVERBS 16:3

The Lord will open the heavens,
the storehouse of His bounty...
to bless all the work of your hands.

DEUTERONOMY 28:12

O Lord, grant us success.
Blessed is he who comes
in the name of the Lord.

PSALM 118:25, 26

I will send down showers in season;
there will be showers of blessing.

EZEKIEL 34:26

May your life in every way
bring glory to the Father
and blessing to you.

If only you could see the blessings God has already prepared for you, and He's preparing your heart *right now* to receive them.

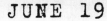

Because Your love is better than life, my lips will glorify You.

PSALM 63:3

Today may you be
surrounded by God's love,
comforted by His grace,
blessed by His peace,
aware of His presence,
and filled with His abundant joy.

You are a shield around me,
O Lord; You bestow glory on me
and lift up my head.

PSALM 3:3

My grace is sufficient for you,
for My power is made perfect
in weakness.

II CORINTHIANS 12:9

JUNE 21

May this day reveal God's love for you...and as you walk in the blessings He gives may you know the fullness of His joy.

Though you have not seen Him, you love Him; and even though you do not see Him now, you believe in Him and are filled with an inexpressible and glorious joy.

I PETER 1:8

This is my prayer:
that your love may abound more
and more in knowledge and depth
of insight, so that you may be able
to discern what is best.

PHILIPPIANS 1:9, 10

Praying you'll know the fullness of God's joy in your day, the closeness of His heart to your need, and the goodness of His plan for your life.

Live a life of love,
just as Christ loved us and gave
Himself up for us as a fragrant
offering and sacrifice to God.

EPHESIANS 5:2

The Lord delights in those
who fear Him, who put their hope
in His unfailing love.

PSALM 147:11

Plant your trust deep in the Lord,
reach out for new discoveries of His
love, and continue to allow Him
to make your life a blessing.

I, the Lord, have called you in righteousness; I will take hold of your hand. I will keep you.

ISAIAH 42:6

The fruit of the Spirit is love, joy, peace, patience, kindness, goodness, faithfulness, gentleness and self-control.

GALATIANS 5:22, 23

May you always know how great
His love is for you, how much He
delights in you, and the wonderful
blessings of belonging to Him.

Blessed is the man who trusts in the Lord.... He will be like a tree planted by the water that sends out its roots by the stream. It does not fear when heat comes; its leaves are always green.

JEREMIAH 17:7, 8

JULY 5

This God is our God for ever and ever; He will be our guide even to the end.

PSALM 48:14

May your eyes be opened today
to the many glimpses
of God's love for you.

You are my rock and my fortress,
for the sake of Your name
lead and guide me.

PSALM 31:3

Since the creation of the world
God's invisible qualities—His
eternal power and divine nature—
have been clearly seen,
being understood
from what has been made.

ROMANS 1:20

May God's purpose lead you
through your day...
May His counsel guide you
in every situation...
May His wonderful love bless you
wherever He leads.

This is how God showed His love among us: He sent His one and only Son into the world that we might live through Him.

I JOHN 4:9

JULY 2

He holds victory in store for the upright, He is a shield to those whose walk is blameless.

PROVERBS 2:7

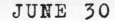

JUNE 30

May the blessing of the Lord
always rest upon you
in hope, joy, and victory!

JULY 1

You give me Your shield of victory,
and Your right hand sustains me.

PSALM 18:35